The book you are reading was provided by a partnership between Rep. Andrea Salinas and the Library of Congress. For more information on Rep. Salinas, visit salinas.house.gov

PEACE PEOPLE

BY ROBYN SHORT AND NANON WILLIAMS

ILLUSTRATED BY LINDSEY BAILEY

GoodMedia Press
25 Highland Park Village, 100-810
Dallas, Texas 75205
www.goodmediapress.com

No part of this book may be reproduced or transmitted in any form or by any means, electronic or mechanical, including photocopying, recording or by any information storage and retrieval system, without written permission from the author, except for the inclusion of brief quotations in a review.

© Copyright Robyn Short and Nanon McKewn Williams 2013. All rights reserved.

Book cover, layout and illustrations by Lindsey Bailey of GoodMedia Press.

The text in this book is set in Futura Medium 16 pt., Amadeus Regular, and Blanch Caps Inline.

Manufactured in USA
Short, Robyn.
Peace people / by Robyn Short and Nanon Williams ; illustrations by Lindsey Bailey.
p. cm.
ISBN 9780991114825
[1. Peace. 2. Peace --Pictorial works. 3. Conflict management. 4. Problem solving. 5. Interpersonal relations.] I. Williams, Nanon McKewn. II. Bailey, Lindsey. III. Title.

JZ5560 .S56 2013
327.1/72 --dc23 2013954424

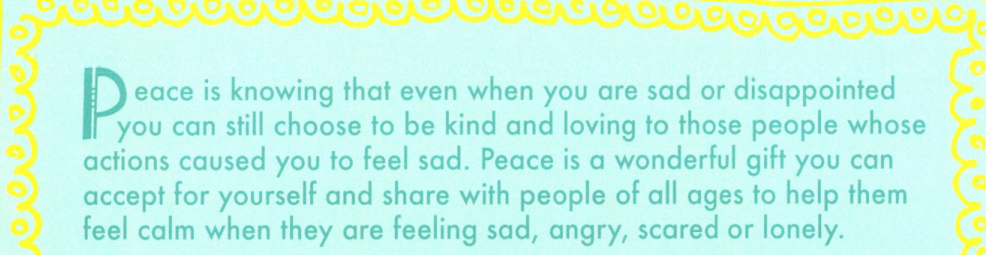

Peace is knowing that even when you are sad or disappointed you can still choose to be kind and loving to those people whose actions caused you to feel sad. Peace is a wonderful gift you can accept for yourself and share with people of all ages to help them feel calm when they are feeling sad, angry, scared or lonely.

By sharing their love, Peace People help others to become their very best by offering kind words and a loving smile. When we share our love, we help to erase the pain that others may feel and help them to feel peace too.

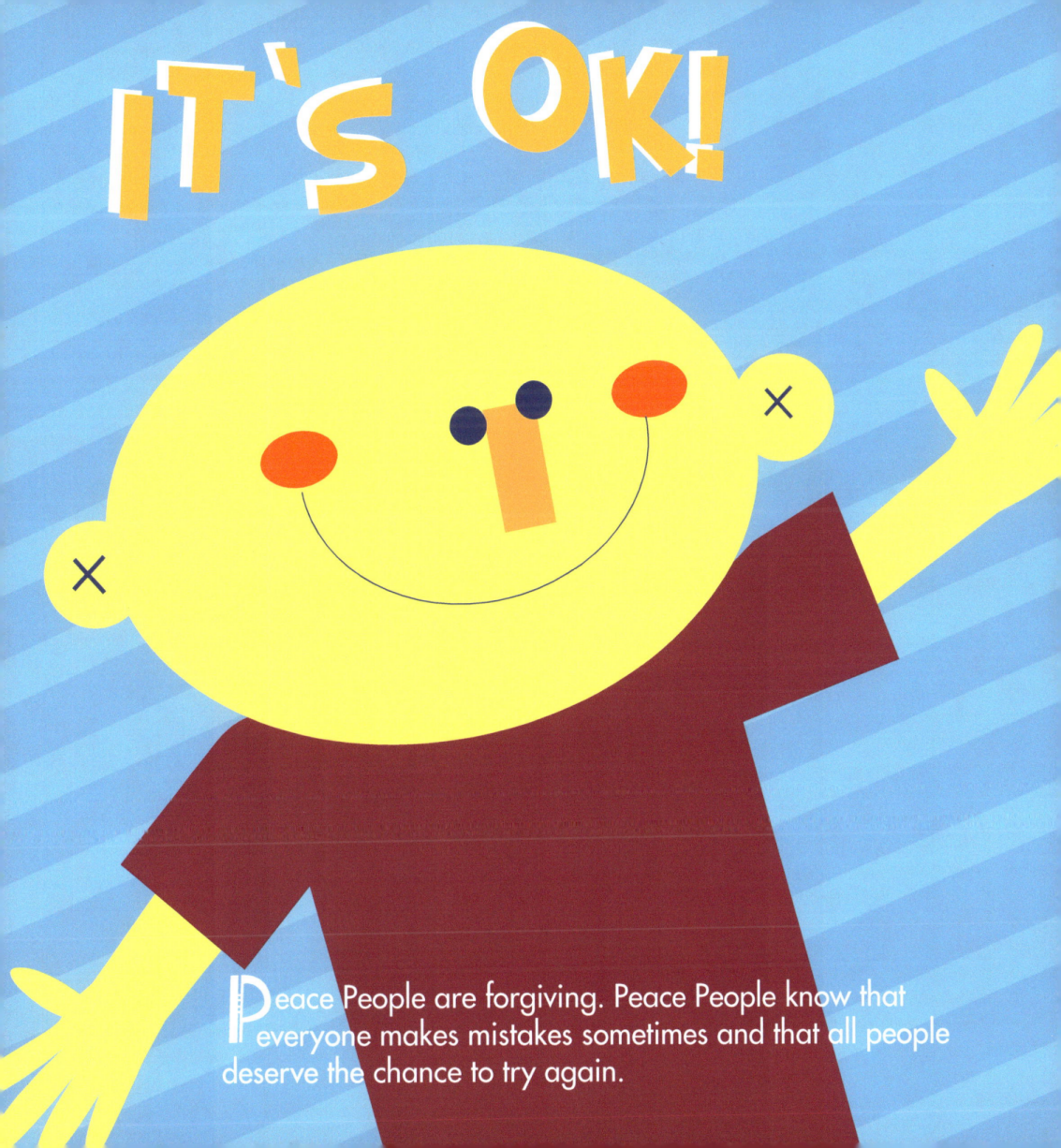

Peace People treat others the way they want to be treated, and we all want to be treated with kindness and love.

Peace People are sharers. They share what they have with their family, friends and everyone who needs someone to share with them.

Peace People love sharing because it makes the love in their hearts connect to the love in the hearts of those they are sharing with. When we share, the peace in our hearts and in our minds grow bigger and bigger.

Peace People are helpers. Every day Peace People wake up and start their day looking for ways to help their family, friends and everyone they see who may need a helping hand.

Peace People help their families with chores at home. They help their teachers take care of the classroom. They open the doors for others and always let them get in line first.

Peace People keep the world around them clean. They help animals to feel safe and loved. And they help to take care of nature by watering plants and picking up litter whenever they see it in the grass or on the sidewalks.

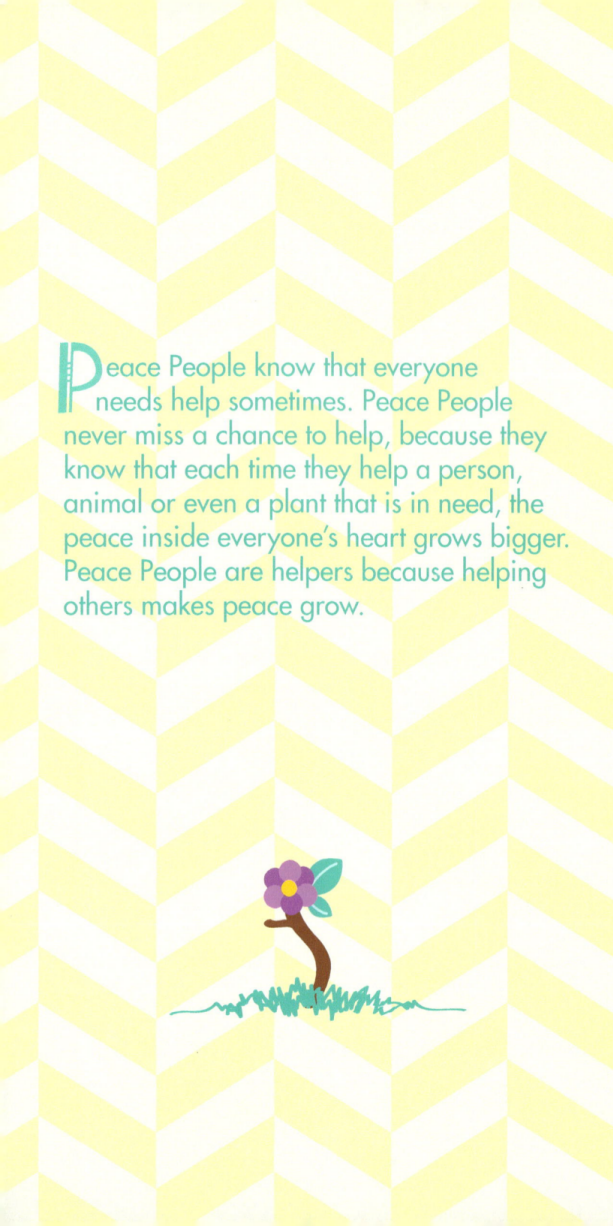

Peace People know that everyone needs help sometimes. Peace People never miss a chance to help, because they know that each time they help a person, animal or even a plant that is in need, the peace inside everyone's heart grows bigger. Peace People are helpers because helping others makes peace grow.

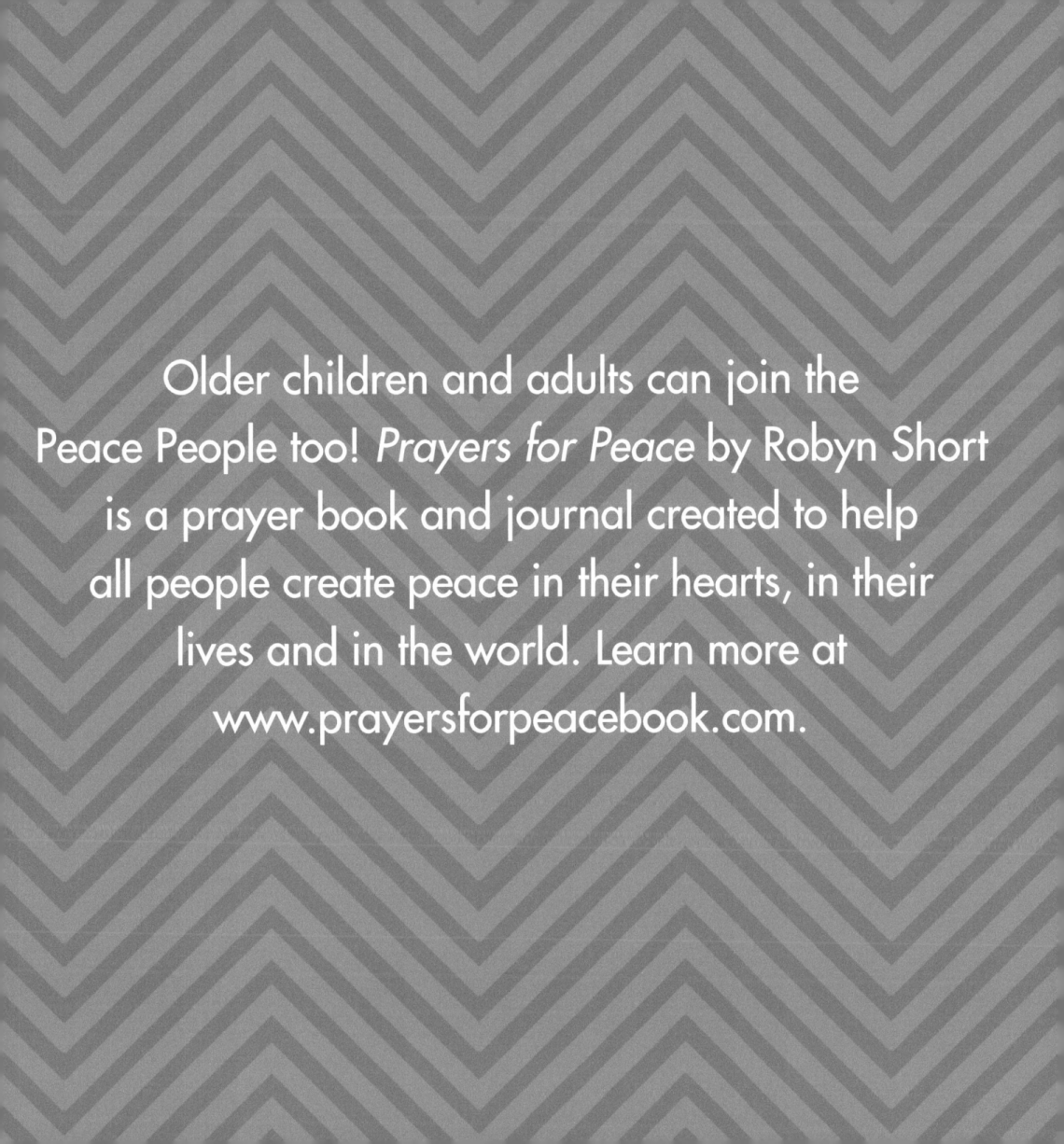

www.ingramcontent.com/pod-product-compliance
Lightning Source LLC
Chambersburg PA
CBHW040027051025
33338CB00005B/31

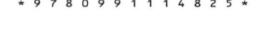